Navigational Tips for Living in an imperfect World

[We're all right as we are, if only we knew it!]

CHARLES BENTLEY PhD
& MARIAN EDMUNDS

First published in 2012 by
NAVIGATIONAL TIPS FOR LIVING
PO Box 6277
Tweed Heads South
NSW 2486
Australia

www.navigationaltipsforliving.com
info@navigationaltipsforliving.com

ISBN: 978-0-9872572-0-8 (PDF ebook edition)
            978-0-9872572-1-5 (EPUB ebook edition)
            978-0-9872572-3-9 (print book edition)

National Library of Australia Cataloguing-in-Publication entry
Author: Bentley, Charles.
Title: Navigational tips for living in an imperfect world [electronic
resource]: (we're all right as we are, if only we knew it!) / Charles Bentley
PhD & Marian Edmunds ; drawings Roger Beale.
Subjects: Self-actualization (Psychology); Conduct of life; Self-
acceptance.
Other Authors/Contributors: Edmunds, Marian. Beale, Roger.

Dewey Number: 158.10835

Cover and text design:
Prue Mitchell, pm3 Art & Design www.pm3artdesign.com.au

Book editing and manuscript development: Laurel Cohn Editing and
Manuscript Development Services www.laurelcohn.com.au

Acknowledgements

We acknowledge the support, hard work and talents of the fine people who have helped in the preparation and production of this book. Thank you. You're all right – as you are!

Contents

Introduction

WE DON'T SEE THINGS AS THEY ARE;
WE SEE THEM AS WE ARE.

ANAIS NIN

MY NAME IS Charles Bentley, and I work toward re-connecting people to the totality of their true being – guiding them to the solid bedrock of who they really are.

My approach to personal and professional development, Unitive coaching, is, as its title suggests, fundamentally different from what has generally become known as 'life coaching'. Instead of being based on any one pre-conceived theory or set of techniques, it provides a safe and secure holistic framework that's individually designed to support you through a creative process of self-understanding and potential fulfilment. It advertises no magical goal, no fantasy destination you are guaranteed to reach. Instead, it takes you on the exploratory journey of your lifetime, through the terrain of your authentic nature.

To live your life to the full, you need to be totally aware of what's happening around and within you at any given moment. Once you've become part of that experience, your entire being – mind, body, and feelings – becomes an instrument for opening up receptive channels of communication between your own true responses and those of the people who share your present environment.

To become personally authentic involves a sea-change in the self. It's about experiencing each event in your life as a present reality, instead of looking at it through the distorting mirror of the past. Rather than trying to influence events from the outside, you find you've become an integral part of them. It's a transforming process to experience the power of the present instead of just observing it. The magical aura it radiates is called charisma – the hallmark of true individuality.

Now read on – what follows is a kind of global positioning system you can use to navigate your own, perfectly valid pathway through an imperfect world.

Charles Bentley PhD

Achieving fulfilment

I HAVE EVERYTHING a person could desire – a beautiful home, a loving partner and family, good friends, and a great career. I should be content with that, shouldn't I? But the truth is, deep down, I'm not content. What's wrong with me?

To find the answer, we need to go right back to the beginning – your beginning. When you're born, the midwife wipes you free of blood and mucus, wraps you in a blanket and hands you to your mother. You're less than a foot long and weigh just a few pounds. You need to be washed and dried, you need warm milk and to be wrapped in a soft clean blanket. It will be some time before you can *do* anything for yourself so you'll rely on your mother (and father) for everything. There's nothing you can give or do in return.

Ideally, you need your parents to accept this, and accept you, without question. Your survival depends on their altruism, or their sense of duty, or their love – or whatever it is that drives them to care for you. Without this, you'll die.

 As babies, we need to be accepted completely for whoever we are or may become. At this point we can't do anything else but surrender to what we hope will be thorough and loving care. As we grow into toddlers, then children and eventually adults, we continue to seek unconditional acceptance and start out on a lifetime's journey: our quest for perfect love. We may occasionally get glimpses of it – sublime moments heard in Mozart's *Magic Flute* or the Beatle's *Revolver* album, or translucent light falling across a painting. Or you'll see it in people – a father and son working together on the family allotment,

or an old woman knitting a hat for her granddaughter, or a little girl sitting in a tree house lost in a reverie. But these are glimpses, and the world is not always perfect like this. And no matter how hard you look, you'll never find exactly what you're looking for, because you  have within you all that you need, if you did but know it.

So then, are you still looking out there for what you need?

I don't think I'm asking for much, really. I just want love, a bit more (or maybe better!) sex, some more money. Sure, I'd like to become a best-selling author, and a house by the beach would be nice. They are things lots of people want, nothing special. Well, maybe a small yacht perhaps? There's nothing wrong with that. That would keep me happy.

There are a few other things you may have already tried – a relationship or marriage, perhaps? Are you still looking for the 'perfect' man or woman?

Well, I don't expect to find the 'perfect' man but it'd be nice to find someone. It would be good too if he had a good job, was clean, and if he made me laugh. Oh, and being able to cook – that would be a bonus.

It's a relief that I don't have to tell you that perfect people don't exist. But nevertheless, medieval ideals of romance are still played out in books, music, and the movies, and continue to influence our contemporary relationships. And those ideals go one giant leap further. Before you're eligible to love, or be loved happily ever after, you're expected to be perfect yourself!

Romantic love is an attachment to projected fantasies based on outdated needs, but real love is different. Real love accepts that our object of desire is a human being and therefore just as fallible and vulnerable as we are.

What about loving my children? Or their love for me? Aren't children meant to be the purest source of joy?

Yes they are – *if* we love them and accept them as they are. And *if* we love and accept ourselves before them, unafraid to be who we are, and to simply do the best we can. We have to be careful, however, not to invest our own dreams in them. They have their own passions and talents far different from ours. We take joy from their presence, and satisfaction in their achievements, and we let them know we are proud of them. We support them when they've come close but are not chosen, or they haven't made the grade. But we must remember it is their success or failure, for them to deal with, and we each have our own successes and failures to process.

How about if I really work towards my goals, and what if I actually get there? Will that help?

Material success may give you a feeling of accomplishment and confidence that you can meet your goals, but it offers no guarantee of happiness, or of being loved. After the adoring crowd that filled the auditorium has dispersed into the night, the performer often returns to a lonely hotel room, or must go out onto the cold street in search of a take-away that's still open at midnight.

It's not love itself that's the problem. It's when you attach to it the condition of perfection that you find yourself in trouble. You already know, in your heart, that you are not perfect. Yet still you may be expecting others to be perfect, and stop loving them if and when they fail to meet your standards. And in the same way, you fail to love yourself – because you're not perfect, because you can't meet a certain standard that you set for yourself.

If you wait for perfection, you may never experience true love, or be truly loved by anyone else. This is the key to everything. If we cannot love ourselves, or others, in a spirit of calm acceptance, then we are setting conditions. Conditional love – 'tough  love' – is not love in its purest sense. We must love ourselves unconditionally because only then can we lovingly develop and nurture those things about ourselves that we wish to work on. The key to discovering your truth and personal integrity is in being able to step back and look at yourself as a whole.

2 The way we see ourselves

WE OFTEN FOCUS so much on one or two aspects of our personalities or physical being that we no longer see our whole selves. Instead, we see a distorted image in which the qualities or features we don't like about ourselves dominate.

Really? Can't they see all the things I want to hide? Don't they see that I could lose some weight? That my hair's not right? Don't they see my big feet?

Quite possibly. However, those things you see as wrong about you are just a part of you, and probably not seen as wrong by others. We may see a monster where others simply see a person. Besides, they are more likely to be pre-occupied by what they feel about themselves!

Of course, you may be able to improve or better maintain the parts of yourself you're not satisfied with through education or training. If you are overweight or unfit, you may be able to exercise  or change your diet to improve your fitness and well-being. But even when you do that, you'll still be the same person. You'll simply be a fitter, or slimmer, version of yourself. That may make you feel better, more mobile, and able to wear a smaller clothes size, and perhaps feel happier. But all of that is only a part of what makes up you as a person.

You need to look at yourself in a different way.

If you can see yourself as the whole person you will see more clearly what role you are playing in events. You will understand very clearly what you are doing, and what you need to do next. It means that you are taking charge of your own feelings and actions. And you won't be laying blame on others for how you are. It is not until we accept and understand ourselves that we can hope to accept and love others.

So I need to change the things about me that I don't like?

No, you need to be able to look at the person you have become from the outside, as it were. It's about understanding what you really are, and looking at yourself with compassion, without judgment. It's about accepting the fact that you're unique.

Oh I know I am. Isn't everyone?

Yes, of course you're unique. There's nobody in the world quite like you, but then, the same applies to everybody else! What makes you truly unique is the DNA structure you were born with – not your personality. You didn't come into the world with a ready-made personality; you've acquired it over a lifetime!

You mean my personality isn't really me?

No, it's a defence mechanism designed to protect, to conceal, the real you. The word personality comes from the Latin word *persona*, meaning 'mask'. Your personality is made up of many different personas, and each one has a specific purpose. Instead of a mask imagine a costume that covers your whole body – a suit of armour that protects you from the outside world.

How do you react to the people you meet and the situations you face? If you look at yourself honestly you'll see an entire wardrobe of costumes or masks that make up your personality. Each is custom-designed to fit a particular situation. But together they make up the one-off collection that identifies you as being separate and distinct from every other person.

I am really starting to get this. So then, can I choose to be whatever kind of person I want to be?

Choice doesn't come into it. Your personality is made up of pre-determined, formulaic ways of reacting to past situations.

The way we disguise ourselves

THINK OF YOUR personality as an assortment of disguises, some of which you wear constantly, almost daily. Others you put on occasionally. Some aspects of our present personality structures are formed in childhood,  others at later stages of our journey through life.

Imagine a schoolboy, a young teenager taunted as he walks home from school. A gang of boys surround him. 'You need to be taught a lesson.' So they hit him, and keep on hitting him. He goes home, and tries to slip inside unnoticed. He tells his mother he fell. He repeats the lie to his father, who says, 'Next time, punch them right back. Come on, I'm going to teach you how to box.'

As he walks home a week later, the boy sees the gang looming and hears them sniggering. Deep inside of him something snaps. He appears to walk right past them and then he turns. They jeer. He stands rock still for a minute, maybe more, and then he walks right up to the leader of the group.

'If you cross me again, I'll kill you.'

Something in his stance makes him seem taller today. The dynamic has changed and in the following weeks the gang not only stops the bullying but each member makes overtures of friendship. But the boy doesn't make friends with any of them. No one bothers him at school again because at the first hint of a threat he cloaks himself with the armour of an aggressive, confrontational attitude. It's the persona he  adopts through life. It works well for fending off threats but it also deters friends and partners.

All through life he continues to try to solve adult challenges with teenage responses.

Some costumes are more appealing than others. A small girl cheerfully agrees to help her mother. She feels good when this happens, and likes the way her mother smiles at her and cuddles her. Throughout her life she readily puts on her costume for helping people. She wears it beautifully and usually it attracts smiles and warmth from the people around her.

Each one of us has a collection of personas to deal with our various life experiences. Taken as a whole, these personas combine to construct a personality and this becomes our identity. Personality and ego are two words with the same meaning. Ego is simply the Latin word for 'I'. Our personal ego forms the protective barrier between the outside world and our inner selves.

So does that then mean I can change my persona, like putting on a different disguise, to suit any situation?

No, not exactly. We encounter problems when we're not aware of the disguises we adopt. It's like being concealed within an opaque cloak. Nobody on the outside can see the true you, and from the inside, even you are not sure of what you truly are.

Think about it like this. An *attitude* is a collection of beliefs about the world, and yourself. Along with your closet full of personas, you have a personal file of attitudes, which relate to your competencies, the goodness or badness of the world, and how you navigate through life. It's a how-to-do-it manual you carry around in your head.

I do hear what you're saying, but I am not fixed in my attitudes. I'm a spontaneous person.

You may think that, but you're not really. Like everybody else, you have your own manual that you look up when you face worrying or unusual situations. How much your attitudes change or remain fixed in the past is up to you! We refer to our manual of attitudes to decide how to behave in any given situation. If your attitude has changed very little in 20 years then your behaviour isn't likely to have changed much either. And if your behaviour doesn't change, the outcome will never change at all.

Picture, if you will, a woman. Attractive, with a home of her own and a career in human resources, she knows a thing or two about people and how they work. She'd love to settle down. When she was 22 she went out to clubs and met men. She sometimes spent the night with one. Occasionally, she still does. Except that now she's getting older, the men are younger and she's craving something different.  The late night encounters don't happen so often, and Internet dating is a minefield. All the good guys seem to be taken. There's been one or two she's been seriously interested in but she doesn't know where to find them anymore.

If she just keeps going and doesn't give up hope, something good is bound to happen. Right?

Well, maybe, or maybe not. We choose our behaviours by referring to our attitude manual. People with fixed attitudes tend to have fixed behaviour patterns. Rather than being open to change and responding in a different way to new experiences in the here and now, they repeat the same behaviour again and again.

So our 22-year-old is soon 37, and she keeps heading out in the hope of finding love, or she stays in. You may be able to recognise similar patterns in your own behaviour. Why do you keep doing the same things over and over? And why then are you so surprised when the result doesn't alter from last time? There are alternatives. You don't need to keep playing the same role over and over.

There's a tendency to get stuck in the past. Attitudes set early in life are familiar, and easy. We play roles we know by heart. There's no need to learn anything new. The problem is, though, that this can limit us to audition only for the more basic roles in life. We confine ourselves to lifetime

performances in insignificant theatres of activity. Our personality structures, laid down a long time ago, seem set rock hard. Even though these structures appear reliable, they depend on a false assumption that life will continue to go on in exactly the same way as always.

But what if some other circumstance crops up, something unforeseen?

Yes, I know. I find it really difficult when things change suddenly. I like to know what's happening. When something unexpected happens I freak out. What should I do in those situations?

You need to be able to improvise. Imagine a stage actor who's rehearsed for a live performance and knows his role inside out. He's not just acting; on stage he *is* that character. But one day the other key actor in the scene trips on the way across the stage and starts to deliver lines from two pages later in the script. What does our actor do? Play along from that line and forget what was missed? Or does he somehow steer his colleague back to the scripted story? And does it really matter, as long as the show entertains and informs?

Sudden changes are inevitable. If you are stuck in a scene of attitudes formed early in life you'll never cope with anything new.

Finding your true role

ACTUALLY, I DON'T want to be an extra all my life. I want to be a star!

In that case, get yourself ready to step into a new role. If your attitudes and patterns of behaviour remain stuck in the past, your eyes will stay focused on an unchanging inner landscape. When you're stuck in fixed attitudes, and attached to one particular version of events, you don't have your eyes open to see what's really going on now.

Can you see what's going on around you right now? Wouldn't it be fun to see something new?

As you become aware of what's going on around you, you'll begin to examine your own fixed attitudes. What are they? And what shaped them?

Now you have a task, something you need to do. It is to bring those attitudes up to date. Make them relevant to today. You've seen people who dress as if they're still in the 1970s – big hair and wide ties – and you know how dated it looks?

Now that you mention it... yes, I think you're right!

It's no different with our attitudes. Who wants their attitudes to be throwbacks to a long-gone era? There's another big advantage of this process. If you can understand your own attitudes and where they come from, it will help you to understand the people you work with and the people you live with. You will start to see where other people have fixed attitudes and set patterns of behaviour. And you'll see they have varying degrees of awareness of this also. With understanding comes an awareness of their feelings and motivations, and with that comes acceptance. It will become easier to accept them just the way they are, with calm empathy and compassion.

Look, believe me, I really want to change, I really do. It's just not that easy, is it?

No, it's not easy. But out there in the world, the real world, the only thing we can rely on – the only constant – is change. It's overwhelming and unstoppable. Yet our response to change, mostly, is to resist it. And very often we reject the idea that change even exists.

Your fixed personality – that is, your ego – acts as a shield to protect you from the perceived threat of change. It's part of our nature to fear change and respond to it with worry and self-defensive mistrust. We deny change exists because we feel threatened by it. We like things to be familiar. So when a new set of circumstances arise, the first thing you're likely to do is to look through your filing cabinet of pre-learned attitudes and patterns of behaviour to find a way to cope. If you can't find something that fits, you go into fight or flight mode.

It's true. I'm really resistant to learning new things. Sometimes, I'd rather just run away and hide.

If you're experiencing tension, anxiety or stress, it shows that an inner conflict is being fought. This is the conflict between your ideal of a constant, unchanging world, and the real world, in a state of flux. Your personality gets taken over by the resistance to change. Much of what you've come to regard as your identity, your 'self' with a small 's', has evolved in its present form due to the resistance.

In a sense, your personality is the resistance! Our personalities prevent us from becoming aware of the true nature of the people we meet, and from accurately assessing the situations in which we find ourselves.  They prevent us from being able to express ourselves authentically.

In fearing change, your perception of the world becomes distorted by the conflict between your instinctive requirements and past experiences.

Literally, you picture the world to fit with your apparent needs. Some of these needs are with you at the present moment, but some are echoes of past needs, clouding the real picture and creating the distortion.

So you're saying I'm still carrying around old stuff that happened years ago, and that I'm still letting it affect me today? Are you sure?

The creative process of perception itself becomes partially replaced by these distorted, fixed pictures, which get in the way of present reality. They represent unsolved issues from the past; the heavy weight of personal baggage you've been carrying around with you all your life; everything you may have done or said about which you still have unresolved feelings of guilt or regret. In other words, your unfinished business. And that's what those old tapes and videos, those re-runs playing in your mind, are all about.

You need to distance yourself from all that stuff by becoming aware of their hidden messages, by looking at them from the outside, by taking a bird's-eye view of all that stuck material.

If I am stuck in all these feelings and memories of past difficulties, how can I become unstuck?

Well, you could use this information I'm sharing with you as a map, or a starter tool-kit. All of the problems associated with stress, coping and dependency are due to various levels of unfinished business, which can be classified according to the degree of resistance involved. Stuff that's only lightly repressed appears in the conscious waking state as a slip of the tongue, or daydreams, or reveries amid periods of rational activity; or as dreams and nightmares. At the next level, the compulsive  acting out of fantasies relevant only to the past prevents the achievement of valid present-day goals. In advanced syndromes, the individual displays irrational behaviour entirely outside the accepted norm, such as delusions or spontaneous hallucinations – the classical symptoms of a 'nervous breakdown'.

That sounds worrying. Am I going to be able to do this?

Yes, you will. It's a matter of needing to focus exclusively on what's presently going on in the real world around you.

Before you can experience true awareness of what's going on in the present, you'll need to  stop acting as if your personal unfinished business from the past is part of the reality of the present. Your resistance to letting go of the past has, over the years, moulded your sense of self, your 'ego' – that is, your personality. Once you can free yourself from wasting your energy on past issues, on unresolved feelings and attitudes from the past, you'll have so much more to give to living creatively and joyfully today.

So how do I do that?

The first step in knowing how to be an adult means letting the child in you express itself.

The child in me? But I'm a grown-up. And I don't have time to play all sorts of silly games.

Listen. This is important. If you can't remember yourself as a child anymore, it means you don't know what your authentic needs are. It also means you haven't truly been you for a long time. If you are always harping back to old desires, or you are obsessed with some place you want to be, someone you might want to be with, or a certain scenario of success, you are not in this moment. You are not allowing yourself to be here, right now, in the same way a child lives in the moment. When did you last take time to simply 'be'?

Well, there was this day when I went out with a friend, and we climbed a hill and sat on a log. The sky was so clear, we sat there for ages. It was beautiful.

When did you do that?

Oh, it was a few weeks, or maybe 3 or 4 months ago.

Like to feel the same way, right now?

Yes, that would be lovely.

Right then. I want you to get comfortable. Are you comfortable?

Yes. No, not really.

This is what I want you to do. Are you ready?

Now, breathe deeply, and become aware of your breathing. Create a kind of rhythm. Next, start to listen to what's going on inside you and around you. You can keep your eyes open, or close them if you prefer. Doesn't matter, either way. Stand back from yourself, and rather than getting caught up in your thoughts, just watch them float in and then out of your head.

Just be. Do it now, if you will. Try it.

In the process of your own personal development, you'll discover how to tap into this state of awareness. The more accustomed to it you become, the more often you will return to the joyful mood that is your birthright, and the more frequently you will be visited by this mood in your daily life.

The worship of perfection

RING THE BELLS THAT STILL CAN RING
FORGET YOUR PERFECT OFFERING
THERE'S A CRACK IN EVERYTHING
THAT'S HOW THE LIGHT GETS IN.

LEONARD COHEN, 'ANTHEM'

ARE YOU CAUGHT between yearning for a perfection you can't achieve, attitudes and ideals that relate to the past? Worship is universal to human nature. And the essence of worship is the desire for perfection.

Everybody worships in one way or another. Today's society advertises all kinds of perfection – a rock hard body, a glittering career, the perfect family, the ideal home. It has become so embedded into our daily lives we're no longer conscious of it. You worry about financial failure, the loss of personal prestige, status and power, and getting old. Do you still constantly strive for perfection? Are you upset when you fall short of reaching it? Do you have a huge bucket list you are trying to tick off?

Yes, of course. There are places I want to see. And what's wrong with having some of the good things in life? I've worked really hard to get those things.

It's fine to want those things, and to have those things. But think about it. In moments of quiet contemplation, you still question what you have lost, and you feel out of touch with things in the here and now. The truth of our lives has nothing to do with what we have, or where we go. It can only be experienced through compassionate and non-judgmental acceptance of the failings of our human condition in an imperfect world.

If we take a long look at the history of civilisation

we'll see that whenever groups of individuals form a society to bring about some standards of morality and ethics, sooner or later a system is implemented to contain the behaviour of its members. Individual spontaneity is replaced by rules set down to perpetuate behaviour only acceptable to the society as a whole. But some of these rules are directly opposed to the instinctual needs of the humans within the society.

So are you saying the rules are making me unhappy? Great! I love breaking rules.

No, it's not the rules themselves – and I can tell you that you don't like breaking them as much as you think! It's the way we respond to them. We end up worrying more about conforming to the rules than deciding for ourselves what best suits our needs. It's not the world at large that societies come to fear, but the instinctive chaos that arises from the functioning of societies. The wish to conform, to be acceptable to others, ends up over-riding the need for authentic self-expression. The body of the individual is taken over by the mass psychology of the community in which she or he is obliged to live. We make a choice, certainly. We choose one half of ourselves, the part that must conform, and reject the other.

Yet still the $64,000 question remains. 'Who are we really?

The $64,000 question! But this is my life. It's worth more than that, surely?

Yes, it is, and yet it's likely you spend it holding back from doing many of the things you want to do. This dilemma of either doing what we truly want to do or conforming to the rules remains a constant source of anxiety to many of us. People who find the fantasies buried in the depths of their chaotic subconscious so unacceptable that they draw back from a full existence into the ivory towers of thought, condemn themselves to a lifetime of doubt. They put themselves into the ultimate double bind: an intellectual trap that they prepare for themselves.

If you really want to explore all there is to being human, you'll need to visit not only the topmost towers of your heady intellect, but the entire castle of your imagination, including the subterranean dungeons where your fantasies lie imprisoned. To live in the lofty regions of thought is to gain nothing but the egotistical illusion of immortality. And to spend your life in fantasies that never see the light of day is to be locked in an unchanging dream that distorts experiences of the present.

Going with the flow

THE PENDULUM OF THE MIND
OSCILLATES BETWEEN SENSE AND
NONSENSE, NOT BETWEEN RIGHT
AND WRONG.

CARL JUNG

MODERN WESTERN SOCIETY celebrates the ego, focusing on individual rights and responsibilities. This is exaggerated to the point that our sole purpose is to 'get ahead'. It's a civilisation in which the ruthless pursuit of self-interest, regardless of the rules, is seen as reasonable. But individualism has led to a limited outlook, a concern with self-gratification, an exaggerated sense of self-importance and a need to be flattered and adored. It makes for an 'upside down' society where the people most loved and respected are the least authentic, and least in touch with themselves.

Those celebrity magazines are just a bit of fun, aren't they? You can check out who's hot on the red carpet, who's dating who and who's in rehab...

We worship the stars of movies and TV but in reality what we're worshipping is the sickness called celebrity. And not only that, we cast the celebrities we supposedly adore as either angels or devils. They are built up, then they fall from grace.

All around us, in the media, in politics, in life, things are either the best or the worst, often lurching from one extreme to the other. And as individuals, we also shuttle between extremes. We see ourselves as being either one thing or the other: strong or weak; a success or a failure; a good or a bad lover, partner or parent. We become unable to see and accept the full range of possibilities of our being.

The more we try to associate with the positive end of the scale, the harder we work to deny the negative. But as hard as we may try, we are never able to fully suppress the conflicts within. Our world is one of endless choices – a Pandora's box of indecisive thoughts, spoken but untested by action. In other words, we get ourselves stuck into the condition known as neurosis.

I don't think I am neurotic. Am I?

All of us are neurotic to some degree with many issues in our lives we have trouble resolving. We work on a 'just in time' basis. We wait for a client or a job and then rush toward fulfilling the implied perfect expectations. In trying to cut costs, businesses make and despatch to order, and employees are expected to be 'always available'. And our leisure time is either spent compensating for the hours at work by making up for lost time or recovering from it. Simply 'being' is not an activity we value. We get bored, easily. Our focus is on productivity. People must always be 'doing' something; and if not we distract ourselves away from 'being' by listening to the radio, watching television, being on the computer, reading, drinking, taking drugs, anything but being with ourselves. We need to open ourselves up to the moment, to ourselves and to those around us. In all of that gorging consumerism, have the excesses given us what we really want?

Well yes, I did want my new car. And I like to update my wardrobe.

Owning the newest designer clothes, fastest car, that sofa, jewellery, make-up and perfume does nothing to extinguish the nagging question: Isn't there more than this? Materialism doesn't deliver the goods.

We live in constant denial of the certainty of our eventual demise and that of those around us. Even the meat we buy in supermarkets is portioned and cellophane-wrapped so that we can deny the death of the animals it came from. Death is a fantasy played out in films or on TV, a far-away thing that happens to people who are 'not like us' in countries we've never been to. Or, closer to home, in a tragedy that could have been avoided, with someone else always to blame.

The world is a dangerous place, isn't it? How do we cope with that?

How? By what the philosopher Heidegger called *dasein*: 'being-in-the-world'. We are only ourselves because we are part of what surrounds us. We have no choice but to engage in it, but our aim has to be to do this authentically. This means truly understanding the people around us, and the events that involve us, by being open, intuitive and spontaneous.

In each of us there is an innate potential for bringing our conflicting parts into an integrated whole. But to experience that elusive integrity,

 you need to let go of all of those egotistical fantasies. Take the risk of living authentically, of showing your true self to other people and to the world. Instead of swimming against the tide of what you really are, breathe deeply, float, and go with the flow.

The problem of choice

MY NECK IS ON THE GUILLOTINE

THE BLADE COMES DOWN

MY HEAD GOES THIS WAY

THE REST GOES THAT

WHICH SIDE WILL I BE ON?

R. D. LAING

INDIVIDUALS OFTEN IDENTIFY with only one polarity. They'll say: *'I am a strong person who can cope with anything that life can throw at me.'* There are opposites at work in human nature. If you project this 'positive' aspect of yourself as representing all of who you really are, you get out of kilter. You fail to recognise those times and situations where it's safe to present yourself as a vulnerable person in need of love and emotional support. You put on a cloak you hope will hide those perceived weaknesses. You identify with a self-image permanently set to positive. This kind of fantasy of personal power, 'success', and invulnerability is the work of the ego. You-as-ego will have you believe you can build a fortress against all the troubles of life.

Alternatively, if you are a person who tends to give yourself a hard time, you will imagine fearful scenarios with no relevance to your own every-day situation, and thereby show a lack of awareness about your positive personal potential.

People, and bosses in particular, often tell me I need to compartmentalise my life? What do they mean? Is that right?

If you compartmentalise aspects of your life you can put on a good act that will go down well anywhere. You can do this quite successfully. But will that help you? It's a very rigid way of going about things. If you choose to identify with any attitude such as 'I'm good', 'I'm clever', 'I'm successful', at the same time, you're not identifying with the corresponding point on the opposite side – *'I'm bad', 'I'm stupid', 'I'm a failure'.*

So if you're saying, *'I'm quite positive',* you're also saying, *'I'm not quite negative'.* And by saying *'I'm extremely positive'* you're also saying, *'I'm not extremely negative'.* The statements are mirror images of each other.

To accentuate positivity and deny the existence of negativity is to fly in the face of common sense. The further you go out in one direction, away from the centre, the further you distance yourself from the opposite. But eventually, what is denied becomes too far away for you ever to see it clearly. In order to build a castle, and climb to the top of it and see yourself as king, you've also had to dig a correspondingly deep hole. You can't make a castle without excavating for the foundation.

I am quite successful, though.

There you go, you're doing it yourself – identifying yourself with success and denying the possibility of failure, eliminating the negative. There's a value judgment involved, where the positive side is seen as a paragon of virtue and the negative side is found guilty on all counts and sent down to rot in a cell. But, as in the words of the song, 'It Ain't Necessarily So'. It's all a matter of opposites. If you balance the negative aspects with the positive, the result is zero – you will be at the centre of self. It's our own value systems that impose artificial divisions upon us.

Our negative, dark, irrational, instinctive and intuitive aspects represent a powerful source of energy that can either become expressed consciously in the real world, or remain deeply buried as denied feelings.

But denying something doesn't mean it has gone away!

8 Projections from the past

LET'S LOOK AGAIN at those old home movies we play in our heads. One of the most common mechanisms we use is *projection*. The way that humans project is not unlike projection at the cinema. An image is thrown up on a screen at some distance where it appears to be much bigger. These old images we carry with us are projected on to other people who are with us now. Sometimes the images projected are so intense that past unfinished business becomes hard to distinguish from reality. But instead of realising we are replaying an old home movie, we attach blame for how we are feeling on to people around us such as bosses, teachers and parents.

Yes, you're right, I've met people who go on and on about something that happened years ago. They never let it go. Why can't they?

Most of us tend to project on to others the inner scenarios that we have denied. It's a mechanism we use to off-load the burden of the stress we feel. This gets more complicated when we've been carrying those stresses for a long time. If we dump denied emotional conflicts we carry from the past, we pay a high price – we lose sight of the other person's true authenticity. They become objects or fantasy-figures rather than people. We no longer see people as they are.

In projecting our past burdens on to people close to us now, we also abuse rather than use the language of communication. We maintain a pretence that negative characteristics exist only in others and are not part of ourselves at all. Even our own internal experiences and feelings get the same treatment. We don't say, *'I have pain,'* we complain that *'It is painful.'* We deny our fears – projecting the feeling out into limbo by saying, *'It is frightening.'*

Oh, so are you saying I project? I thought it was only other people who did that.

Most people project more often than they are generally aware. It happens whenever we encounter people or situations that remind us of unfinished business from our past. Our internal projector starts whirring and all of those pent-up fears, resentments, longings for love – all the stuff we hoped we'd stored away for good in the archives of fixed attitudes – start rolling again. Every time another person pushes the button of one of our fixed attitudes, we stop functioning consciously. Instead we become emotionally involved with our own denied fantasies. We begin to act out a melodramatic role in an old and entirely irrelevant scenario.

You can easily identify the projective processes

in everyday interactions.
Whenever other people say
things such as, *'You're really
annoying!'* or *'You shouldn't do
that!'* you'll begin to see they
are not taking responsibility for
their own negative attitudes.
They're trying to dump them on you. It's not your
responsibility to correct other people's attitudes.

**But what if they are really annoying? Or is it only me
who thinks that?**

See how easy it is to start projecting? What
you're learning here will help you to keep your
emotional distance when this happens, as it's
bound to do, often! It really is their problem, not
yours. But it's important you become aware of
your own tendency to project a negative attitude.
It gets in the way of you doing your job.

My job? What might that be?

Yes, your job. As a responsible user of interpersonal
dialogue you are committed to using language

that reflects your total dedication to honest and direct communication.

In other words, it's how you say things.

For example, instead of saying, *'You're really annoying'*, try saying, *'When you do that, I get annoyed'*.

Don't say, *'You mustn't do that'*, but try instead to tell it like it is: *'I feel bad when you do that'*.

We've all seen when we were young how all kinds of projections from seemingly more powerful people got through the half-built defences of our personality. If you detect any tendency toward this in your own personality, start to deal with it. You can do this by admitting the long-denied needs of you-as-the-underdog. Share them with your partner or a sympathetic friend!

So what are you saying, exactly?

What I am saying is that you, me – all of us – need to own our emotions. We need to not pick on someone else or give them a hard time when it's really us who's grappling with our feelings.

Some people do not project their insecurities on to others but turn them back on themselves. They incorporate into their own behaviour and reactions the attitudes and expectations of significant and powerful figures whose love, approval and acceptance they've yearned for in the past. The technical name for this is *introjection*: the means whereby individuals deny the existence of parts of their authentic nature seen as negative, bad or lacking in virtue. This is less common than projection.

Hmmm, what about those people who never show their feelings about anything?

They do exist, certainly. It sounds as if you know some yourself! It's a tall order to contain personal conflicts of rage, anger and fear but some people try to do this because they feel revealing their inner battles is dangerous or reveals a lack of control. They keep their feelings permanently out of sight – blocked out of conscious awareness. It's easy to recognise this kind of fixed attitude by the habitual use of phrases such as, *'I hate myself'*,

or, *'I get angry with myself'*, or, *'I tell myself not to'.* There's an on-going fight within the personality structure, with an aggressive top dog on one side and a powerless underdog on the other.

Projection and introjection are similar in that their fixed attitudes see a personality that seems divided against itself. The person becomes his or her own worst enemy. Some people, however, will do anything to avoid division. They go along with the crowd for a better life. They have personality structures that don't develop fully even when they become adults. With few opinions of their own, they take on board the fixed attitudes of the society in which they are immersed – like a sponge soaking up water. It's a one-sided arrangement to agree with the majority view. Going along with the crowd – the technical word here is *confluence* – gives them a sense of security they feel they will never achieve for themselves.

So do you mean they end up being like a chameleon?

Yes. People become confluent in the hope that mass acceptance will bolster their fragile sense of personal worth. Unfortunately, instead of getting the approval, recognition and high status they were looking for, they inevitably find they've become an anonymous face in the crowd. Individual integrity is relinquished, which sooner or later leads to a loss of real contact with others and an increasing sense of alienation. The feeling associated with this denial is either projected outward as resentment or anger or turned inward as self-pity or guilt, by the process that goes under the name of *retroflection*.

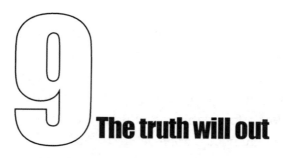

The truth will out

'...THERE IS NO NEED TO REMEMBER WHAT I SAY:
THERE IS NO NEED TO UNDERSTAND WHAT I SAY.
YOU UNDERSTAND; YOU HAVE FULL UNDERSTANDING
WITHIN YOURSELF. THERE IS NO PROBLEM...'

SHUNRYU SUZUKI

YOU CAN RECOGNISE the symptoms of inner turmoil both in the way people speak, and in how they are physically. The signs are within you, in how you express yourself and in how you feel. Each of us uses mechanisms to hide our authentic thoughts and feelings rather than to communicate them. If you're honest with yourself you'll recognise some of these at work within your own personality structure.

That's a bit alarming isn't it? I don't want to reveal everything I'm thinking.

Relax! There are some easy ways to bring hidden and fixed attitudes out into the open and to clarify your own dialogue with other people. They are not hard-and-fast techniques to be learned by heart, but a foundation on which you can build your own individual approach.

I'll give you some examples. It's not that difficult to deal with confluence. This divides the world into two camps – 'Us' and 'Them'. You can always tell what side this type of fixed attitude is on.

'We' (our kind of people, the in-crowd) are always right, and 'they' (the outsiders) are invariably wrong! Give-aways in every day speech of a confluent person are phrases that show mass fixed attitudes that have been swallowed whole. Examples include *'One expects...'; 'Everybody knows...'; 'People always say...'*  People to whom confluence is important ask what lawyers call 'leading questions' – that is, questions about your opinions. They do this to find out what side of the fence a person is on without expressing their own prejudices first and risking rejection.

In future you will be able to identify this kind of ambiguous loaded question as soon as you hear it. One way of turning the tables on it is by saying, 'I'd be interested to hear what you think'. Another useful and non-confrontational way to get past a confluent attitude and to the denied authenticity behind it, is to ask a direct open question. This might be something like, *'What do you feel now?'* or, *'What do you want now?'* or, *'What are you doing now?'*

What's the point of doing that? How will that help me?

The aim, as always, is to re-establish contact with the real self–the person behind the mask. Constant practice in using a few simple skills of listening, observing, empathising and speaking will help you recognise negative attitudes in yourself, and in others. It will also help you to form effective channels of interpersonal communication.

Whenever possible, express your thoughts or feelings by making statements instead of asking questions. Instead of asking *'Do you need?'* say, *'I have a feeling that you need...'* When you ask for information, make sure it concerns facts you need for the job in hand. Asking for opinions may lead you into a minefield of hidden projections! Focus on what's really happening at the moment by using the present tense. For example, *'Right now, I'm glad you're here!'* rather than, *'I'm disappointed you didn't come last Tuesday.'*

Avoid confluence by using the first person singular – *'I feel'* – which is a true personal statement, instead of saying *'It feels...'*, or, *'We/they/everybody feels...'* which is a false general attitude.

Substitute the word 'and' for the word 'but'. For example, 'I want to talk to you but I find it difficult' is an introjected problem revealing a fixed attitude. Instead say, 'I want to talk to you and I find it difficult,' which is a clear, honest admission of the present situation.

So it's better to say 'and' instead of 'but'? I have never known there is such a big difference.

Take personal responsibility for your projective processes. Instead of saying 'What you just said made me feel sad,' say, 'When you said that, I began to feel sad.'

Respect the authenticity of your own intuitive feelings as a person quite apart from your role or your profession. As a general rule keep your opinions to yourself! But keep in mind there will be times when it's appropriate to share personal reactions with other people. It's important to consider if it's in the other person's best interest and if it's entirely free of any negative intent on your part!

So, how I say things can make a huge difference?

Hold on, that's only part of it. You need to know how to listen as well.

Paying attention

PEOPLE ALWAYS TELL me I am a good listener.

Listening is an integral part of the process called attending. When you really attend to another human being, your authentic self will stop paying attention to your own internal 'static'. Then you won't be hearing the projected, interjected, retroflected and confluent messages from the various departments of your acquired personality. Only then are you free to detach yourself from the demands of the ego, and focus a powerful beam of pure awareness entirely on the outside world.

Once you've attained that state you can attend completely to what the other person is saying. Listening is an art. Like any other form of creative endeavour, the more you practice it, the more proficient you'll become.

But it's really hard to concentrate. Thoughts keep jumping into my head.

Don't worry if at first you find it hard to completely free your mind of all the background noise of your thoughts and feelings. Just be aware of what's going on and then make a conscious decision not to get attached to it.

Pure attention is a state of calm relaxation; a holiday taken by the real you, away from the distractions of your personality. You've heard the expression 'a train of thought'? Well, you don't need to get on board. If you do, you'll get carried away. Watch it go by, and keep your focus on the reality of the other person. Pay close attention to what is being said, without interruption. After you think they have finished speaking, wait a few seconds more. What people say after a pause usually turns out to be important!

As you learn to listen, you'll become increasingly aware that in a typical conversation, what a person chooses to tell you may not always be relevant to the particular issue being discussed. When you are listening to whatever is said, remember to watch out for double messages. Your intuitive reaction won't let you down. Trust your gut response and you'll hear the true meaning behind the words.

OK. I hear you. What do I do next?

The next step is learning to respond to what you've heard. You may find it useful to first sum up in your own words the gist of what was said to you, to see if you got it right. Then, wait for more feedback, and repeat the process until you are both satisfied. What you're looking for is complete clarity. Don't become emotionally hooked. When someone projects something on to you that affects your feelings, in any way, just breathe a little deeper and, literally, watch yourself. Accept the feeling but always remember acting upon it will take you to an unreal place.

There are several ways you can get to the real

meaning behind whatever it is that is being said to you:

> Repeat what you have heard to be sure you've accurately understood the underlying message. So you might restate what someone has said. *'Let's make sure I've got this right? Do you think I actually feel superior to you as a person? Is that what you mean?'*

> Request that the other person re-phrases a statement in order to explore and/or to emphasise important aspects of the message. *'You seem to be saying you're quite pessimistic about your prospects in this situation. Is that really the way it seems to you?' Or 'You don't sound at all confident about passing your exam!'*

These are just a few of the many feedback techniques that can help clarify the interactions between yourself and the people you meet in your various roles in life.

To really listen is to allow the other to express him or herself at some length without interruption, so that you can identify an underlying theme that ties together seemingly unrelated statements.

Here's an example of how you might check that out. *'All right then. So, on the one hand, you think you've got what it takes to succeed in work but on the other hand you believe your boss is prejudiced against you. Am I understanding you correctly?'*

But I still don't get it! How does becoming a better communicator help me to view the world differently, or to tune in to my real self? How on earth can I do all of that?

Let me explain...

Living in an imperfect world

WE DO NOT SEE THE WORLD
AS IT IS: WE SEE IT AS WE ARE

THE TALMUD

WE EXPERIENCE THE world in four different ways: using perception, intuition, thinking and feeling. Perception and intuition distil meaning from events in the outside world or from flashes of insight from the unconscious. With judgments and decision-making based on information received through perception and intuition, we think and feel. All of these determine what we can see, hear, smell, taste and touch.

Perception is our interpretation of what's going on around us at any given moment.

So, if someone else were sitting where I am right now, what would they see and hear? Would they hear the rain on the roof too? Would they feel the cushion propped behind their back? Would they taste the lemon cake I am eating?

It depends. We perceive only those elements of the world that are relevant to our inner needs at any given time. Perception is only our interpretation of 'reality'. Someone else sitting in the same place as you are may see, hear and smell the world quite differently.

Intuition comes from within. It's the ability to know something without any clear idea of how you reached that conclusion. This happens to all of us. When you meet someone new, you may have a 'gut' reaction. Your intuition tells you something about them. You will be instantly accessing the personal store of information buried deep inside you. Or you will delve deeper still, into a part of you that is the sum experience of everyone who's lived before you.

Our intuitions are stored as images in an ancient part of our brain – the limbic region. Within that are blueprints of human survival encoded in the human DNA and passed down through the generations.

Whenever you come across a situation in the real world that threatens your survival or security, your intuition will never fail to come up immediately with the best possible response. There's no threat it hasn't come across before. The optimum response to every bad thing that's happened in the history of the human race is filed there.

It's good to know that I've got the ability to respond instinctively to any situation.

In an emergency, thinking takes too long – it just gets in the way. And by the time you've worked out a plan of action, it's probably too late! Thinking is a divisive process. Abstract thought splits things right down the middle. Before we can start to think, talk, or write about any concept we have to cut it in two. Like the computer that mimics it, human logic works on the binary system. We need to choose one or the other – either the yin or the yang so that we can take appropriate action. This choice implies uncertainty, and that's where all the problems start.

Your mind never stops thinking. Sit back for a moment, and listen to the chatter. Listen to the voices in your head. We all have stories we are telling ourselves, and it's up to us how we choose to interpret these stories, and whether we let them affect our actions.

So I can decide how my story unfolds? That could be fun!

It can be hard to silence this chatter, to have moments of stillness where you can simply be. This conversation can be so over-powering that you lose touch with the other ways in which you experience the world.

Feeling is completely different to thinking. Take a moment now to examine how you feel. It is a purely emotional way of interpreting the world. It mediates what's going on in the 'real' world according to very basic assessments of pain versus pleasure, and pleasant versus unpleasant.

You know all about feelings – the adrenaline rush of excitement when in danger; the red mist of anger when you're wronged; elation when you've achieved a goal and received recognition; sadness at loss. Feelings can be so strong that you see the world through a fog of them. Of course you've noticed that when you're in high spirits, the world is full of sunshine and smiles. And when you're low, reality appears gloomy and grey.

I'm beginning to see what you mean now. It's like there's a filter for how we feel? And how we see the world depends on the filter?

Well, something like that. In the modern Western world we're taught to rationalise, to rely heavily on our thinking. We're trained to master our feelings. But you can't bury your feelings. Nor should you try to. Feelings are an essential key for unlocking a deeper understanding of what's really going on. You can't hide away from the world. You're an integral part of it, not separated from it. And there is no need to resist it, fight it, or to try to change it.

You can only hope to truly know yourself by embracing and accepting all of the ways in which you experience the world, and accepting yourself as being part of it.

So are you saying we see what we need to see when we need to see it?

You are getting better at this! If we look at flames, or passing clouds, or the patterns of tea-leaves at the bottom of a teacup, every one of us will see different images. Perception scans the foreground to find an image that is personally meaningful. And what we recognise as significant at any given time is always highly influenced by our past conditioning and unsatisfied needs. More often than not, what we perceive in the present consists of older, projected elements. We yearn for gratification of our suppressed needs and overlook or ignore important information right in front of us. Instead of absorbing the outside world by a process of osmosis, we see only those elements that fit in with a fixed and outdated view of the world.

Once we become aware of the relationship between need and perception and start to trust the truth of own experience, we find there is no Reality with a capital R: no Absolute, no Given. There is only the passing and subjective reality of our own awareness.

It's like adjusting our own personal viewfinder to suit the conditions?

Yes, absolutely.

Nobody's perfect!

MAN IS THE ONLY
CREATURE WHO REFUSES
TO BE WHAT HE IS.

ALBERT CAMUS

HUMAN YEARNING FOR ideal role models has been expressed through many forms of religious worship. But as Western society has become more secular, the longing for perfection has shifted focus to material aspirations. In many human relationships, one person unconsciously endows qualities of perfection on another. In the language of romance, this is called falling in love. In psychological terms, it's called transference. In any relationship that assumes an unequal power balance between the two people involved, the 'lesser' will typically project their longed-for ideal on to the 'greater'. They will attribute to them ideal or god-like qualities.

Transference has been called the projecting of a perfect picture upon an imperfect screen. This can also happen in relationships with professionals we seek out for their specialised skills. We can invest in them a belief that they have answers we cannot find.

Do you mean like when we put someone on a pedestal?

In the traditional professions, such as law and medicine, the boundaries are relatively clear-cut, with expertise being assumed within the confines of that particular field. However, in some interpersonal relationships the boundaries may become blurred, and transference is certainly something of which you need to be aware.

When perfect qualities are attributed to one person by another, the honesty of the dialogue between the two people will be compromised or distorted. If the other person starts to believe that he or she possesses god-like qualities, they may also start to believe they are not subject to the normal rules that apply to mere mortals. It also means they are looking through a distorted viewfinder both at themselves, and others.

Come on! Are you kidding? Who really believes they're a god?

You don't have to look far – just look in the media! The vast majority of the 'celebrities' in our present-day culture suffer from a virulent form of ego-mania recognised in ancient mythology as hubris – the assumption of mere mortals that they possess god-like attributes. We are human and must face others not as their betters, but as their equals.

Once we gain insight into the truth of ourselves and other human beings, we accept and become committed to present reality and the inevitable imperfection of life – and of all who live it. And in that very imperfection we will see the truth and beauty of the individual and the possibility of change.

It seems we are all perfectly imperfect, or is that imperfectly perfect?

The ability to be who we really are – to act intuitively from our true centre – is the greatest gift we can give ourselves. To get in touch with our authentic being is to recognise our real needs and desires and to be able to express them to others. Once we unlock the door to intuitive knowledge, we will come to understand the strength of our individual power. Once we widen the horizon of our consciousness and develop our intuitive potential, we are better able to know and express ourselves, and to communicate effectively with others. Our material, career and personal achievements are much more likely to become 'realised', in the true sense of the word.

It all sounds perfectly sensible, and very wise too. And I believe you, honestly I do. But the thing is, even though I am a grown-up and should know what I'm doing, there are days when I feel utterly lost, when I have no idea where I am going.

Living in the here and now

WE SHALL NOT CEASE FROM EXPLORATION
AND THE END OF ALL OUR EXPLORING
WILL BE TO ARRIVE WHERE WE STARTED
AND KNOW THE PLACE FOR THE FIRST TIME.

T.S. ELIOT

YOU SAY YOU'RE lost, that you've lost direction. OK. Just imagine, then, that you are lost – really lost! – in the place which you are experiencing as being in the here and now. Even though you're standing still, you're thinking, 'I wonder in which direction I should go?' or 'Which one of the infinite number of possible paths should I take?' There are 360 degrees in the compass but you don't know which one to follow because you don't know what you're aiming for, never mind where you're going or even which direction it is. But still you're trying to go towards it.

I know I am! Which way should I go?

I can't tell you that. But this is what I can say: The reality you need to accept now, and I mean really realise, is that if you know where you are right now then you're not lost, because you're already home!

So you're saying if I know where I am, I can't be lost?

There are two ways of living.

You can say, 'These are my aims and goals and I'm going to go hell-for-leather to achieve them.' This is the unexamined life.

Instead, you can say, 'Let's look at where these aims came from, because they've taken me to a place in the present where I don't want to be.' As soon as you stop aiming for will-o'-the-wisp goals in life, you can take a fresh and perceptive look at how you've arrived where you are right now. And when you do this you'll be free to explore where your authentic nature will take you. This beats rushing along in an endless race to reach imaginary goals. Instead, your life becomes a joyful journey where things you never imagined become possible.

But don't we still need goals? What's wrong with wanting to achieve something?

Yes, goals are important. But often we are pushed hard to achieve goals, by coaches, or parents, or figures of authority – some well meaning, others less so – towards striving to achieve our 'perfect' goal.

But please beware, future goals are illusions, dreams about what we'd like to achieve, or where we'd like to be. The place that we are aiming to be is no more real than the place we are right now, or at any given moment. If we are not careful we can waste a great deal of our precious time in pursuit of something that never has existed, nor ever will.

The view you see now is different to the one you will see in five minutes. Even if it hasn't changed much, it will have changed in some way. Life is not a heartless slog down a motorway. It's more like a meandering river. You may set out wanting to go to such and such a place on the riverbank, even though the current may be against you.

I'll just keep rowing and rowing until I get there. Yes?

No! Relax, there's nothing you need to do. Just go with the flow, let the river take you where it will, and watch what happens, moment by moment. Even though you don't change, the vista before you is changing every second. Different things come up; and every moment has a different potential to the next moment. And that's what life is – just celebrating the scenery as it unfolds before you.

The real journey of life is not to a far-away place, but a journey back into your authentic self. There you will find a deep understanding of your attitudes and behaviour that are fixed in the past. You will see your yearning for perfection for what it is, and that you perceive the world differently according to your present mood.

Through acceptance of your mortality and the discovery of the joy of living in the moment, and by re-connecting with your intuition, you'll tap into a bottomless wellspring of authentic impulses and creativity.

14 Finding your way home

TO LIVE YOUR life to the full, you need to be totally aware of what is happening around and within you at any given moment. Personal authenticity is all about experiencing each event in your life as a present reality, instead of looking at it through the distorting mirror of the past. Once you've become part of that experience, your entire being – mind, body, and feelings – becomes an instrument for opening up receptive channels of communication between your own true responses and those of the people who share your present environment.

To become personally authentic involves a sea change in the self. It's a shift from the personal to the transpersonal; from the ordinary to the extraordinary. Instead of trying to influence events from the outside, you find you've become an integral part of them. It's a transforming process: experiencing the power of the present instead of just observing it. The magical aura it radiates is called charisma – the hallmark of true individuality.

The loving compassion that we crave is already within ourselves, if only we knew it. How can we recognise it? We can do ourselves a favour and stop trying to change ourselves for the perceived better – for a change! There's no need to get better. We're all right as we are. Yes! Did you get that?

You're saying, I'm all right as I am. There's nothing wrong with me? Did I hear that correctly?

Yes. Emphatically yes! There's nobody out there with the power to tell you otherwise. Acceptance of this simple truth is within your own reach.

By definition, this little book will be insufficient to express the essence of the authentic human experience of 'being-in-the-world'. The very words in which it is written are the instruments of a rational attempt to describe an integrated state that can only be experienced. It will always be necessary to trust your own basic instincts to find a practical, safe and reliable way of working toward the only worthwhile goal in life: the attainment of a lasting sense of peaceful fulfilment and calm self-acceptance.

But please take comfort from this. There is no challenge, internal or external, that can't be successfully navigated by someone who has an integrated understanding of, and relationship with, his or her authentic self.

And there's nowhere you need to worry about reaching, because you're already home. You're there, but you don't know it. Not yet, but you will.

The motivation

BY MARIAN EDMUNDS

ONE DAY I read an interview in a newspaper with Dr Charles Bentley, a personal development coach, and I liked what he said.

It was 1999, and I was living and working in London. I had it all – a job at one of the world's leading newspapers, a big home with garden, travel, a marriage, a son, a loving family, and many friends. Yet, I felt something was missing. I had no idea what that was.

For one thing, I could never leave work and its politics at the office. I'd be worried about understanding the topic; about commissioning writers for articles; about being short on copy – like trying to stretch a single bed sheet across a double bed. If there was too much it felt like an exercise in slashing and burning, then I'd have to deal with the egos that didn't like to have their words cut.

The peskiest and most time-consuming thing of all to deal with for me was people.

People: who noted your minute of arrival in the office but never your hours of overtime; who counted the time till retirement by the hour; who spoke politely to their colleagues then were snide the moment they walked away. I was not so foolish as to imagine they weren't snide about me either. It wears you down after a while.

But there were also some wonderful people and there is a certain buzz you get from the proximity to things. You're not passively watching news events, you have the chance to do something useful, to gather the most comprehensive information you can in the time available, and to present the facts as known up to that moment, in a logical and intelligent fashion. When a big story breaks, and the day's news list must be scratched and drawn up again, and everyone is under the pump, and must work together, there's a kind of magic that comes into the equation. At such times you can't imagine anything outside of that.

Mostly it's not like that. More often it's about checking that there's a circumflex on Côte and no 'e' on Azur before running down three flights of stairs and to the other end of the building to show the pages to the editor.

Look, don't get me wrong, circumflexes matter! And I was, more or less, doing what I'd planned to do. A girl who'd grown up in the town upon which the film Muriel's Wedding was based, was working for one of the most respected newspapers in the world. I'd made it!

Was I happy?

I was always running; for the train in the morning, up and down stairs, across the newsroom. Then, at the end of the day I'd run past the pubs, markets, cathedral, across a treacherous road, and up a dusty grey side street and along the platform to reach the 5.32 train. And in the carriage I'd crumple myself into the available space, in a smelly pond of fatigued jackets and loosened ties. At my stop, I'd push my way out and run again, overtaking the cars idling reggae, their drivers and engines fuming in the peak hour.

Breathless, I'd knock on the door of the home where my son was being minded, relieved to escape post-6pm overtime charges. Then I'd trudge home pushing the stroller laden with my bag, my son's bag, my shopping, to start on the evening routine of bathing and dinner. And through it all and for the rest of the evening, my deadlines and the events at the office would be still be on my mind.

I had achieved my ambition after all yet I didn't have any feeling of triumph. On the one hand I felt unrecognised for my ability, and on the other, I doubted whether I had any right to be there.

So tentatively but with hope, I called Charles Bentley's number. It seemed from that first conversation that we might work well together. And we did. After a very short time I had a stronger sense of where I was and what people around me were up to as well, even the people who'd been difficult to deal with. I not only changed the way I worked, including my hours and activities, but I began to feel differently about it all. Best of all was that it was relatively simple to do. Charles did not give me a long checklist of daunting tasks to be completed by our next meeting. Our conversations were inevitably surprising and enlightening. And oddly, the days when I'd wake up thinking, 'I'm ok, I probably don't need this session, there's nothing to discuss', would turn out to be the days I'd experience an epiphany.

I also never gave a damn about office politics again. What I learned during that time with Charles has stayed with me, calming me at times of stress, and helping me to remember that I am all right – as I am. It seemed to me that this information might help other people too, so in this book the many things he shared with me have been shared with you.

About Unitive coaching

BY CHARLES BENTLEY

THE UNITIVE APPROACH to personal development coaching enables you to become totally aware of your uniqueness, while at the same time remaining completely in touch with the world around you. It works on all four aspects of the totality of being human. At the rational level, it makes you aware of patterns of behaviour that are past their use-by date. At the psychological level, instead of transferring your power to figures of authority, you are empowered as a unique individual, with self-knowledge and personal authenticity. At the emotional level, it reconciles spontaneous feelings with intellectual insight. And at the higher, integrated level of intuition, it provides a platform for personal development in the areas of imaginative transcendence and creativity.

This approach is entirely individualised. It throws away all our pre-conceptions and focuses entirely on the unique reality of each individual and each session. Each time is different, and each time new things are seen. We think of it as a journey by coach. You don't know exactly what you will see on the journey or what you will find. Neither do we. It doesn't give you all the answers. But you don't need them. It gives you a calm space for reflection. And it gives you a route to finding solutions for your own problems, simply by using the forms of expression and pre-existing resources relevant to you. When you gain insight into your own internal processes, you can make the changes you need to transform your life.

The Unitive approach takes on board the on-going nature of individual change and development. It does not offer an escape from the inevitable watersheds of life. Nor does it, or can it, offer avoidance of suffering. But that's OK. You see, there is no challenge, internal or external, that can't be successfully navigated by a person who has an integrated understanding and relationship with oneself.

Be wary of pre-fabricated, bullet-point 'training' procedures offering to take you on a fantasy trip to a land of instant gratification. Unitive coaching works toward the deconstruction of previously conditioned learning, and the negative and guilty feelings it brings up about supposed personal inadequacies – feelings which are, at the basic level, self-inflicted.

We're all right as we are. Acceptance of this simple truth is within your own reach. This is the most powerful and central function of Unitive coaching – to show you the way towards this liberating insight. Truly life-changing and effective coaching is concerned with 'being-in-the-world' – that is, the fact that we are not separated from the physical world in which we find ourselves at any given moment but, instead, are an integral part of it.

The Unitive approach understands that problems do not exist in the real world, but are internalised within each of us. It acknowledges that once you get in touch with who you really are, you don't have to worry about what you should do, ought to do, and must do. It's only then that your activities will become free of conflict – spontaneous and authentic. The wide scope of Unitive coaching facilitates the innate ability that lies dormant within everyone – to integrate present conflicts between individual need and lifestyle roles and to cope with, and learn through, the process of change.

About the authors

CHARLES BENTLEY PhD

Charles's unique and comprehensive Unitive approach to personal development coaching has evolved as a result of his many years of experience in the field of human potential. Over the past three decades he has worked in the UK, Europe and the US as a professional agent of change with many international companies and a wide range of institutions.

Based in central London, Charles has a coaching clientele that includes media personalities, entrepreneurs and many professionals in the business and corporate world, media and the arts. He is often quoted in the national quality media as a recognised authority on personal and business coaching and has appeared on BBC TV's Omnibus, Channel 4 TV, ITV1 and BBC Radio 4. He can be found via lifecoach.co.uk and lifecoachuk. com.

MARIAN EDMUNDS

Marian is a writer and journalist based in Australia. A BSc (Hons) Economic & Social Policy graduate of Birkbeck College, University of London, Marian was on the editorial staff of the Financial Times in London for 15 years. Her work has appeared in many major newspapers as well as specialist travel and tourism publications. Marian is among a distinguished group of contributors to the literary travel anthology, city-pick New York. She writes for clients and mentors people through the fiction writing of their own stories. In recent years, she has become drawn to fiction, and is moving towards her goal of being a novelist. She can be found via thewritingbusiness.com.

We're all right as we are, if only we knew it!